BABYSITTING

Babysitting
ACTIVITIES

FUN WITH KIDS OF ALL AGES

by Wendy Ann Mattox

Consultant: Beth Lapp
Certified Babysitting Training Instructor

Capstone
press

Mankato, Minnesota

Snap Books are published by Capstone Press,
151 Good Counsel Drive, P.O. Box 669, Mankato, Minnesota 56002.
www.capstonepress.com

Library of Congress Cataloging-in-Publication Data
Mattox, Wendy Ann.
    Babysitting activities: fun with kids of all ages / Wendy Ann Mattox.
    p. cm.—(Snap books. Babysitting)
    Summary: "A guide for pre-teens and teens on age-appropriate activities for entertaining children while
babysittting"—Provided by publisher.
    Includes bibliographical references and index.
    ISBN-13: 978-0-7368-6461-9 (hardcover)
    ISBN-10: 0-7368-6461-X (hardcover)
    1. Babysitting—Juvenile literature. 2. Amusements—Juvenile literature. 3. Play—Juvenile literature.
I. Title. II. Series.
HQ769.5.M38 2007
649'.10248—dc22   2006001731

Editor: Becky Viaene
Designer: Jennifer Bergstrom
Photo Researcher/Photo Editor: Kelly Garvin

Photo Credits: Artville, LLC, 19 (raisins); Capstone Press/Karon Dubke, cover, 4–5, 10 (crayons), 10–11, 12–13, 14–15, 18–19, 26–27, 29 (all); Capstone Press/TJ Thoraldson Digital Photography, 7; Corbis/zefa/S. Hammid, 28; Getty Images Inc./ Iconica/Nick Daly, 23; Index Stock Imagery/Chris Lowe, 9; PhotoEdit Inc./Myrleen Ferguson Cate, 16–17, 25; SuperStock/ Kwame Zikomo, 21; Wendy Ann Mattox, 32

1 2 3 4 5 6 11 10 09 08 07 06

Table of Contents

CHAPTER 1

Planning for Fun

Congratulations! You've just landed your first babysitting job. But how are you going to entertain the kids for 3 hours?

Have no fear! This book will give you lots of ideas to keep the children you are babysitting from getting bored. Whether caring for a baby, toddler, or older child, you'll learn what activities will keep kids of all ages entertained.

Pick babysitting activities that you enjoy too. But skip watching your favorite TV show. Your job is to keep the kids happy and busy. Knowing what activities are best for kids of certain ages will help you and the children you babysit have a fun-filled time together.

Playing with Babies

Babies are cute and cuddly. But it may seem hard trying to entertain someone so small who can't talk. Don't worry. Babies are usually easy to entertain.

Babies learn by listening, looking, and touching. Shake a rattle. Babies enjoy toys that make noise. Read short texture books and help babies touch textures, like a soft bunny tail. Colorful board books are also a good choice. A baby can hold onto the thick, strong pages of board books without ripping them.

Helpful Hint

Babies put everything in their mouths. Make sure that all toys are too big to swallow. Also check toys for sharp points or detachable parts.

Entertaining Ages 0-1

For young babies, simply changing their scenery keeps them from getting bored. Move the baby from his playpen to your lap. You can also place him in a baby swing, a high chair, or a stroller. You can even vary a baby's scenery without moving her. Place a mobile over her. She'll enjoy watching the colorful mobile slowly spin. It will also help improve her vision.

Music is also a good choice for babies. It helps improve their listening skills and often calms them. Carefully hold the baby and dance slowly to the music.

Older babies need more action and excitement. They enjoy repeating actions. Singing and simple games, like pat-a-cake and peekaboo, are some of their favorite activities.

PHYSICAL DEVELOPMENT OF BABIES

Although every baby is different, this list shows when most babies do certain things.

3 MONTHS: grab a rattle and smile

6 MONTHS: roll from back to stomach

9 MONTHS: crawl, stand with help, and play games, such as pat-a-cake

12 MONTHS: walk without help, dance to music, and say a few words

CHAPTER 3

Keeping Toddlers Busy

Toddlers are on the go non-stop. They may enjoy listening to a book, but don't plan on reading the whole thing. Toddlers have short attention spans and like to change activities often.

Make sure you're well rested to watch a toddler. Keeping up with such an energetic youngster can be tiring. Children at this age are curious and love to explore with their new skills of running, walking, and climbing.

Toddlers are often happiest while playing with simple items that aren't even considered toys. They may enjoy playing in an empty box or diving into a pile of pillows.

You can help toddlers learn. Teach them problem-solving skills by helping them use shape sorters or stacking toys. Work together to stack blocks and make a tall tower. Crash! Toddlers will love knocking down towers even more than building them.

Show toddlers how to express their creativity by scribbling with crayons. Watch carefully while they color. Make sure they color on the paper instead of the table and walls.

11

Entertaining Ages 1-3

Short games and finger plays are favorite activities for toddlers. Songs and finger plays help children improve memory skills and allow them to learn while imitating. Sing "Where is Thumbkin," "The Eensy, Weensy Spider," and "If You're Happy and You Know It."

WHERE IS THUMBKIN?

Where is thumbkin, where is thumbkin? (Hands behind back.)

Here I am! (Bring right hand out from behind back with thumb up.)

Here I am! (Bring left thumb up and out.)

How are you today, sir? (Wiggle right thumb as if it's talking.)

I am fine, thank you! (Move left thumb as if it's answering the left thumb.)

Happy day! Happy day! (Clap.)

Repeat for other fingers: pointer, tall man, ring man, and pinkie.

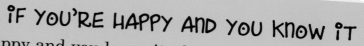

IF YOU'RE HAPPY AND YOU KNOW IT

If you're happy and you know it, clap your hands. (clap twice)

If you're happy and you know it, clap your hands. (clap twice)

If you're happy and you know it, then your face will surely show it.

If you're happy and you know it, clap your hands. (clap twice)

Alternate "clap your hands" with fun verses such as "hop on one foot" or "stick out your tongue."

THE EENSY, WEENSY SPIDER

The eensy, weensy spider climbed up the waterspout. (Connect thumbs with pointer fingers to make spider.)

Down came the rain and washed the spider out. (Use fingers to show rain pouring down and washing spider away.)

Out came the sun and dried up all the rain. (Hold hands above head to show a sun.)

And the eensy, weensy spider climbed up the spout again. (Make spider again with fingers.)

13

Fun for Preschoolers

Preschoolers love attention. From showing you their new karate moves to making a mask, preschoolers are proud of things they can do without help.

Preschoolers especially enjoy making things for their parents. Drawings, collages, and other projects don't have to be perfect. Mom and Dad will love anything their child makes!

Preschoolers can also use their creativity and imagination by pretending. Take turns pretending to serve and eat food at a restaurant. Place stuffed animals around the house and pretend you're on a trip to the zoo. Ask the child to come up with an imaginary situation and then prepare to pretend.

Art lets preschoolers use their creativity and imagination. Children at this age should use washable markers, safety scissors, and non-toxic white glue. Try some of the art projects below with the preschoolers you babysit.

SiMPLE ART PROJECTS

Paper Plate Lion Masks

Color paper plates yellow and fray the edges with a scissors. Cut out eyes and glue the mask to a craft stick. ROAR!!

Collages

Cut out pictures of your favorite foods from old magazines. Glue them on a sheet of paper.

Sack Puppets

Decorate a paper sack by gluing on yarn for hair and buttons for eyes. Then hold a puppet show!

Entertaining Ages 4-6

Preschoolers often enjoy playing independently. Play next to them. Encourage their efforts, and help them with harder tasks. Race small toy cars and trucks. Zoom! Play with plastic toy animals, or create something with play dough. These activities all help improve a child's small motor skills.

Most children enjoy the excitement of playing with new toys. Try bringing an activity kit filled with age-appropriate toys. Not sure what to put in the kit? Check out these ideas.

Bring an Activity Kit

You can fill your activity kit with fun and exciting supplies, such as:

* Play dough
* Books
* Board games
* Small toy cars and trucks
* Art supplies

GREAT GAMES

Games teach preschoolers how to take turns and follow directions. Both of these games begin by having players line up on one side of the yard with a caller on the opposite side.

Mother May I?

The person who is the mother (caller) gives instructions, such as take two giant leaps, to one person. If the player forgets to first ask, "Mother, may I?" she must return to the starting line. The first player to touch the mother becomes the new caller.

Red Light/Green Light

The traffic light (caller) begins by facing away from the players and yelling "green light." Next the caller turns around and shouts "red light." Players can't move during a red light, or they must go back to the beginning. On a green light, players run or walk and try to tag the caller first. The first person to tag the caller becomes the new caller.

CHAPTER 5

No Couch Potatoes Allowed

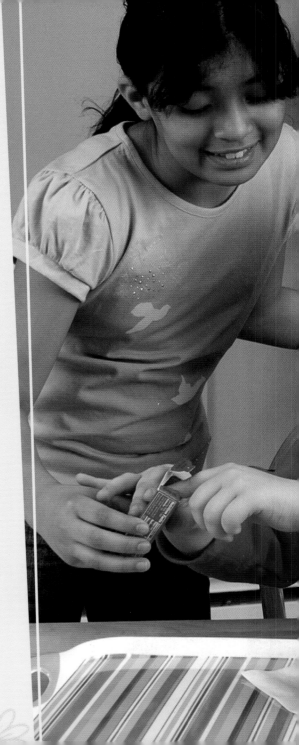

TV, computer, video games—older kids could spend hours with these machines.

Although it's good to give kids over age seven some time alone, don't give them too much. Check with parents to find out how long kids are allowed to use the TV, computer, or video games.

Be prepared with suggestions for things, like games, that you can do together. Older kids are proud when they do well at board games, such as Monopoly, Scrabble, or Life. They love to strategize.

Older kids also enjoy learning new skills and being helpers. Teach them to prepare recipes, such as ants on a log. If you have permission to use the oven, teach how to make cinnamon breadsticks.

KID FRIENDLY RECIPES

Ants on a Log
Fill pieces of celery with peanut butter or cream cheese. Top with a few raisins.

Cinnamon Breadsticks
Roll refrigerated breadsticks in 2 tablespoons (30 milliliters) sugar and 1 teaspoon (5 milliliters) cinnamon. Twist together and lay on a cookie sheet. Bake as instructed on the package.

CHAPTER 6

Let's Go Outside

Most kids would rather play outside than inside any day. Whoosh! You catch a giggling child at the bottom of the slide. The choices of outside activities are endless.

Outside activities help children use energy, stay healthy, and improve their large motor skills. Use hula hoops and other large toys to create an obstacle course. Toss a football, shoot basketballs, or play freeze tag.

After being active, kids might be ready for more mellow activities. Offer to push them on a swing. Let them use sidewalk chalk to draw a picture on the driveway. Suggest a game of hide-and-seek or follow the leader.

FUN OUTDOOR GAMES

Follow the Leader

Players follow the person who is the leader and copy what the leader does. For example, the leader may skip around a tree and summersault across the grass.

Freeze Tag

Players are chased by the person who is "it." If touched, they are frozen and must remain in place until another player touches them to unfreeze them.

Activities for Boys & Girls

Boys and girls enjoy many of the same activities. But you likely won't get a boy to play with dolls, or a girl to pretend she's a pirate.

Boys love being active. Sports such as soccer, basketball, and baseball are usually favorite activities. Boys also like to pretend many different things, including that they are firemen, policemen, and pirates.

Alternate wild activities with quiet activities to avoid boys getting too excited. A fun, yet calm, indoor activity is building objects, like dinosaurs, with small blocks. Boys also enjoy playing with toy cars and trucks, especially ones that make noises.

Sugar and Spice and Everything Nice: Activities Girls Enjoy

Girls often enjoy activities that involve less action and more imagination. Do you have any old dress up clothes or shoes? Bring them with you and pretend to have a fashion show!

Get ready for the fashion show by doing another thing girls enjoy—putting on makeup. Pretend to put makeup on each other, or use washable makeup. Later, style each other's hair and paint fingernails.

Most little girls also enjoy other imaginative activities, such as tea parties. You can make signs or menus for the tea party. Want more tea party guests? Dress up dolls and invite them.

Bedtime: Quiet Activities

Kids would love to stay up all night and play high-energy activities like tag. But it's your job to slow things down.

Before bedtime, choose quiet activities, like reading and coloring, so the children have time to unwind. Let children know when it is almost time to get ready for bed. If you only have 20 minutes to play, remind them every 5 minutes. Don't rush the bedtime routine. Allow at least 45 minutes for the children to wash up, eat a snack, and brush their teeth.

When the kids are ready for bed, offer to read a book. Let the children choose a short story that their parent usually reads to them before bed. Keeping a familiar bedtime routine will help them feel more comfortable without their parents. You can also sing the children a song, such as "Twinkle, Twinkle Little Star," before leaving the bedroom.

27

Ready, Set, Time for Fun!

From playing peekaboo to racing toy trucks, you're an exciting babysitter. Prepared with many simple, safe, and fun activities, you'll have no trouble keeping kids of all ages busy. So get ready to build, color, play, sing, and pretend. Let the fun begin!

Checklist:

Planning for Plenty of Fun

Before you arrive at a babysitting job, think about the following questions. If you don't know the answers to these questions, ask the children's parents.

✓ **What ages are the kids you'll be babysitting?**

✓ **Do you know what activities are appropriate for these ages?**

✓ **Do you know what the kids like?**

✓ **Do you have activities that would interest both boys and girls?**

✓ **Do you have ideas of activities to play inside or outside?**

✓ **Are the items in your activity kit safe for babies and toddlers?**

Glossary

collage (cul-LOJ)—a variety of pictures or words cut out from magazines and glued onto a piece of paper

large motor skills (LARJ MOH-tur SKILS)—the abilities needed to control the large muscles of the body for walking, crawling, and other activities

obstacle course (OB-sta-kuhl CORSE)—a group of objects used to race through or around

small motor skills (SMAWL MOH-tur SKILS)—the abilities needed to control the small muscles, including the hands and fingers, to pick up objects

Quick Tips

* Always get permission from the child's parents to cook or play outside.

* If you take the children outside, make sure they have appropriate clothes on. On colder days they may need jackets and hats.

* When playing outside, tell kids what you expect. Set boundaries, such as staying in the backyard.

* Two activities kids really enjoy are looking through family photo albums and watching family movies.

* Remember to switch the items in your activity kit to keep it fresh and exciting.

Read More

Braman, Arlette N. *Kids Around the World Play!: The Best Fun and Games From Many Lands.* New York: J. Wiley & Sons, 2002.

Kuch, K. D. *The Babysitter's Handbook.* KidBacks. New York: Random House, 1997.

Press, Judy. *ArtStarts for Little Hands!: Fun & Discoveries for 3-to-7-year-olds.* Charlotte, Vermont: Williamson, 2000.

Sadler, Judy Ann. *The Kids Can Press Jumbo Book of Easy Crafts.* Toronto: Kids Can Press, 2001.

Internet Sites

FactHound offers a safe, fun way to find Internet sites related to this book. All of the sites on FactHound have been researched by our staff.

Here's how:

1. Visit *www.facthound.com*

2. Choose your grade level.

3. Type in this book ID **073686461X** for age-appropriate sites. You may also browse subjects by clicking on letters, or by clicking on pictures and words.

4. Click on the **Fetch It** button.

Facthound will fetch the best sites for you!

About the Author

Wendy Ann Mattox began babysitting at age 12. Her love for children continued to bloom as she grew up. As an adult, she is now married and the mother of four lovely daughters. She is a preschool teacher and freelance writer. She writes articles and books for children and about children.

Wendy believes that babysitting can help prepare anyone to become a better parent. And babysitting may even lead a person into an exciting career in teaching children or writing. It did for her!

Index